Ballads

and

Court Dances

of the

16th and 17th Centuries

Harp Solos and Duets
arranged by Deborah Friou

Selections from the recording **Renaissance Muse** for
non-pedal and pedal harp

Thanks To:

Trustees of the National Library of Scotland for permission to use selections from the **Straloch Manuscript** (MS. 349).

Edinburgh University Library for selections from the lute book of **Sir William Mure of Rowallen** (MS. La III 487).

Cover illustration from Giovanni Boccacio, *Des cleres et nobles femme* (MS. 33, f. 24r).

Used with permission of the Spencer Collection, The New York Public Library; Astor, Lenox, and Tilden Foundations.

All arrangements by Deborah Friou

Music typesetting by Michael Pierceall

Cover art direction by Patti Benner

The music in this book may be heard on the recording *Renaissance Muse*, available on CD and online.

Friou Music
P.O. Box 157
Brunswick, ME 04011 U.S.A.

ISBN 978-0-9628120-5-7

Introduction

The music in this book was selected from ballads and court dances of the 16th and early 17th centuries. During this time, music was a highly developed form of recreation for a public with growing resources and leisure time. The harp was a popular instrument of the period, illustrated in Michael Praetorius' Syntagma Musicum (music encyclopedia), played in Scottish castles, and painted with illustrious people of the day, including King Henry VIII. It was often considered to be interchangeable with lute and keyboard.

Michael Praetorius (1571-1621) was a German composer, organist, and music publisher. He published a vast quantity of work, including a volume of instrumental French dance tunes entitled Terpsichore, after the Greek muse of dance.

Claude Gervaise, a French composer and arranger, edited or composed the Danceries, a series of volumes of dance music published by **Pierre Attaingnant**, whose business was located in Paris on Rue de la Harpe.

John Dowland and **R. Askue** were Elizabethan composers and lutenists. Many popular English ballads of the day were arranged for solo lute.

Two important sources for the tunes in this book were the earliest lute manuscripts from Scotland. The Straloch Manuscript (1627) includes extracts from the lute book of **Robert Gordon Straloch**, a Scottish cartographer.

Sir William Mure, of Rowallen Castle, a Scottish poet and amateur musician, compiled a small lute book in 1616. Both books contain courtly dance music in the French style as well as traditional Scottish tunes.

Table of Contents

About the Dances:

*The **bransle**, (branle, brawl) was a very popular group dance of the 16th century, executed in a circle or line. It is derived from the French word branler, meaning to "swing" or "sway."*

*The **courante** (corranto, currant) is derived from the French word courir, meaning "running" or "flowing." This dance originated in the 16th century and was described by Arbeau as a dance with jumping movements and a variety of evolutions.*

Gaillardes were moderately quick, lively dances in triple time. The word is derived from Italian for "vigorous," "robust." The dance was executed with exaggerated leaps.

*The **almande** was a dance in moderate duple time, which first appeared around 1550. It was described by Thomas Morely as being "a more heavie daunce than the gaillard" and having "no extraordinarie motions."*

Jigs were popular English dances of the 16th century in 6:8 time. It is suggested that the name is derived from the old English word jocus, denoting a farcical ballad. Names of well-known jigs as "Kemps Jig" and "Slaggins Jig" refer to the famous clowns of English comedy.

*The **canarie** was a European dance that came to Spain from the Canary Islands. It is in quick 3:8 or 6:8 time with dotted rhythms. Arbeau, in his book Orchesographie, describes the dance as "gay, but, nevertheless, strange and fantastic with a strong barbaric flavor."*

*A **lilt** was originally a word of Scottish origin, meaning to sing in a clear light tone with cheerful rhythm. Lilts were used to accompany solitary tasks and were usually sung by women.*

Canarie I

Arr: Deborah Friou

Straloch Lute Book
1627

By courtesy of the National Library of Scotland

Ladie Ann Gordon's Lilt

Arr: Deborah Friou

Straloch Lute Book
1627

Gracefully

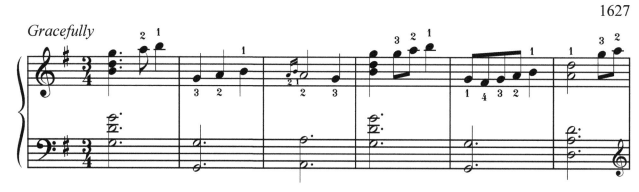

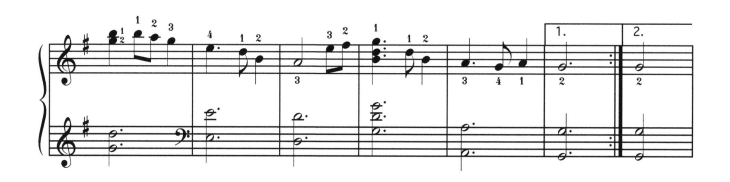

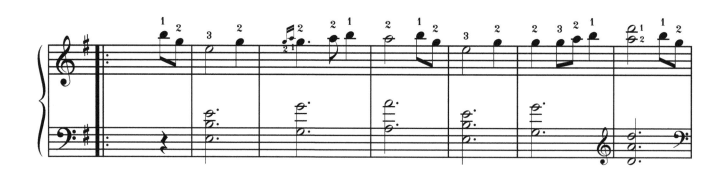

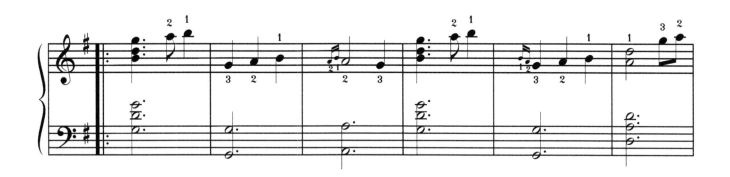

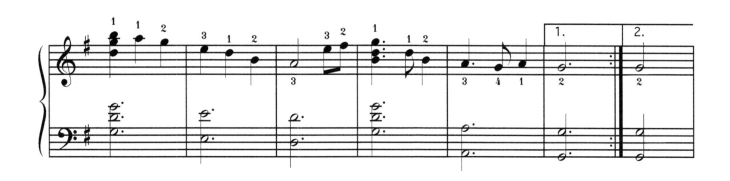

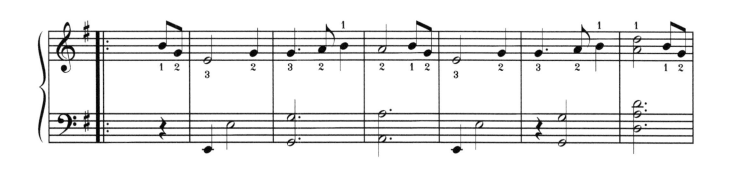

Canarie II

Arr: Deborah Friou

Straloch Lute Book
1627

With Spirit

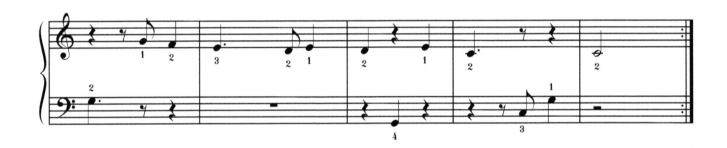

Damp with
flat palm.

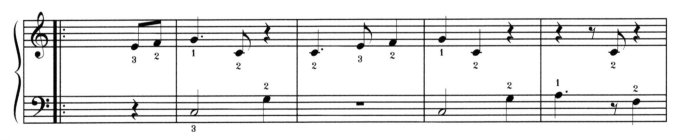

By courtesy of the National Library of Scotland

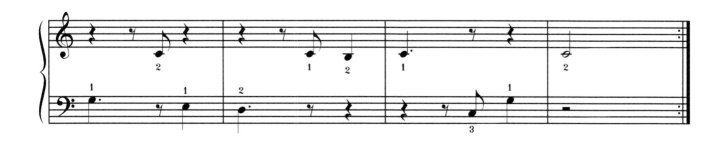

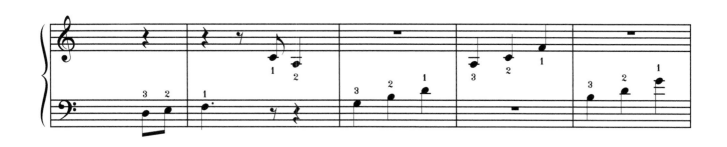

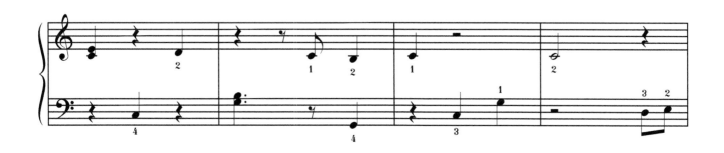

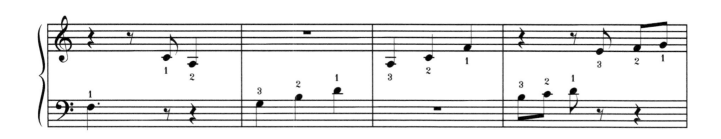

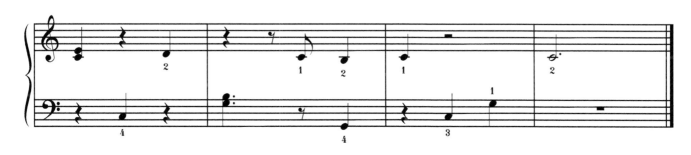

A Daunce

Arr: Deborah Friou

Straloch Lute Book
1627

Very Quickly

By courtesy of the National Library of Scotland

11

Currant

Arr: Deborah Friou

Rowallen Lute Book
1620

Quickly

By courtesy of Edinburgh University Library

Corne Yairds

Arr: Deborah Friou

Rowallen Lute Book
1620

By courtesy of Edinburgh University Library

Cabot

Arr: Deborah Friou

Rowallen Lute Book
1620

By courtesy of Edinburgh University Library

15

Scots Tune I

Arr: Deborah Friou

Rowallen Lute Book
1620

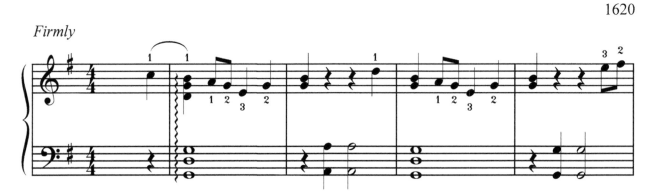

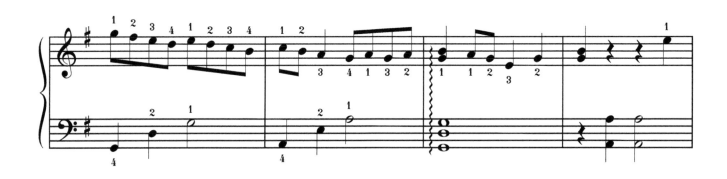

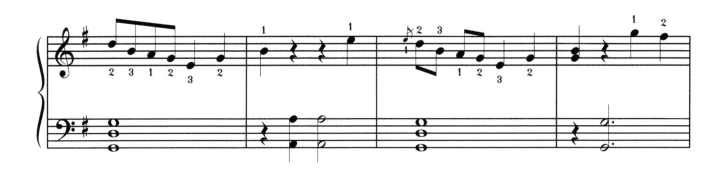

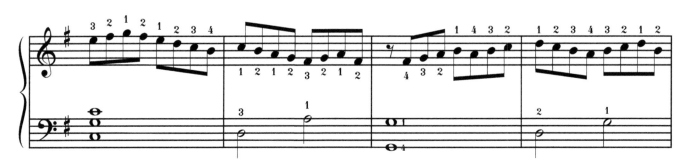

By courtesy of Edinburgh University Library

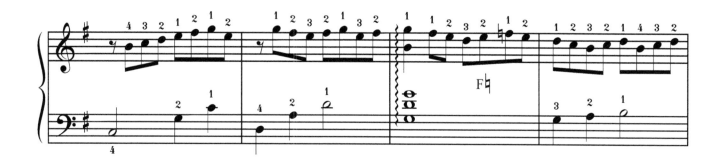

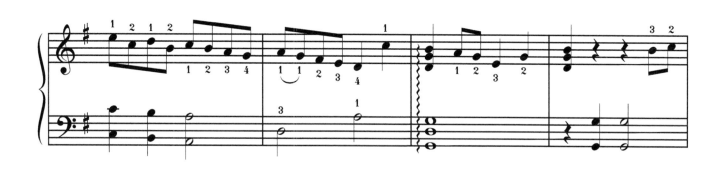

17

Scots Tune II

Arr: Deborah Friou

Rowallen Lute Book
1620

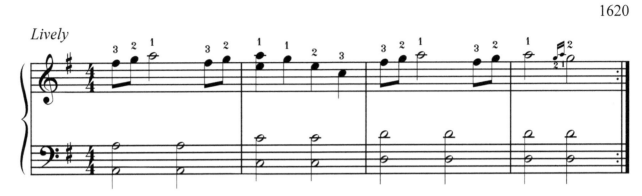

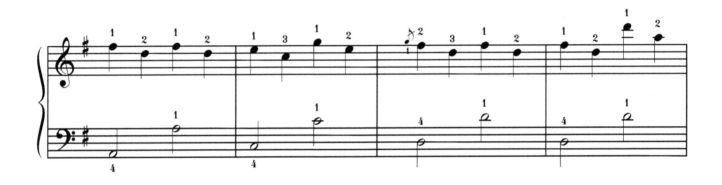

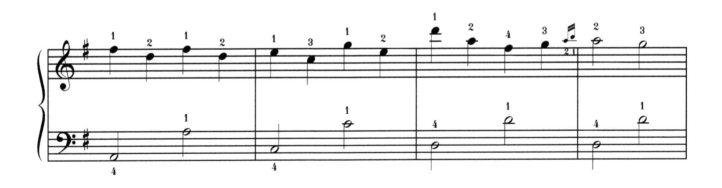

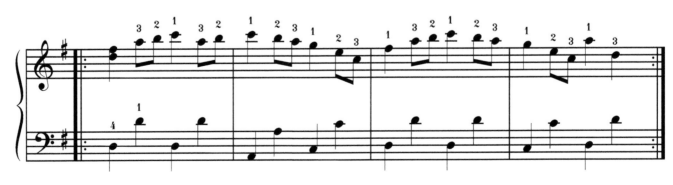

By courtesy of Edinburgh University Library

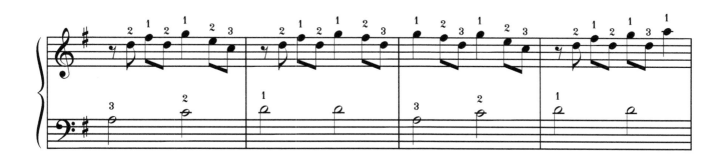

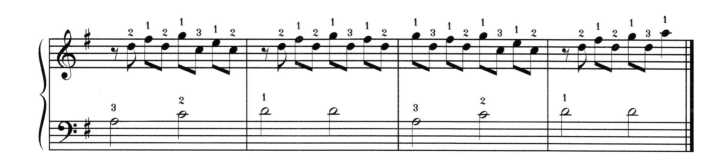

I Long for Thy Virginitie

Arr: Deborah Friou

Straloch Lute Book
1627

Wire-strung Harps: Dampen strings as indicated

Freely, with Feeling

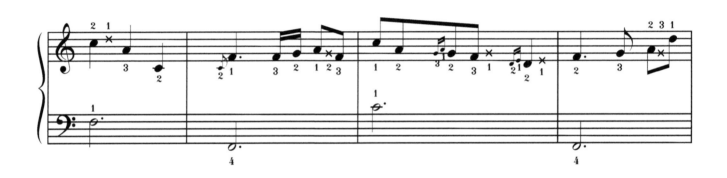

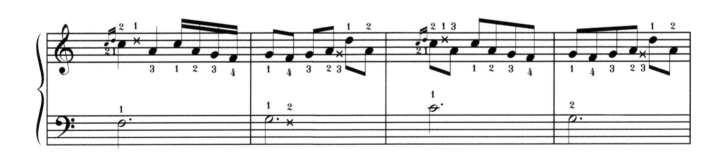

By courtesy of the National Library of Scotland

A Scots Tune

Arr: Deborah Friou

Wire-strung Harps: Dampen strings as indicated

Expressively

Rowallen Lute Book
1620

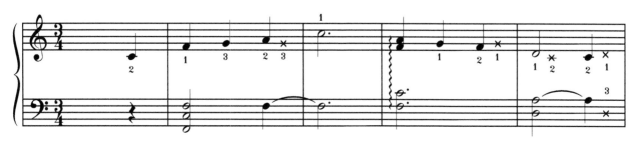

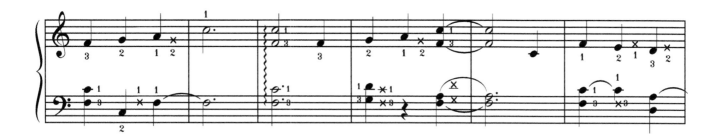

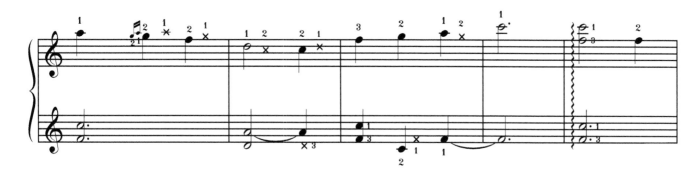

By courtesy of Edinburgh University Library

Spyenelit Reforme

Arr: Deborah Friou
Lever Harps: Set middle F♯
Wire-strung Harps: Dampen strings as indicated

Rowallen Lute Book
1620

By courtesy of Edinburgh University Library

Almande IV

Arr: Deborah Friou

Lever Harps: Set middle F♮

Stately

Claude Gervaise
16th c.

24

Gaillarde

Arr: Deborah Friou

Claude Gervaise
16th c.

Moderately

Three Ravens

Arr: Deborah Friou

Lever Harps: Set low C♮

Expressively

Trad. English
16th c.

26

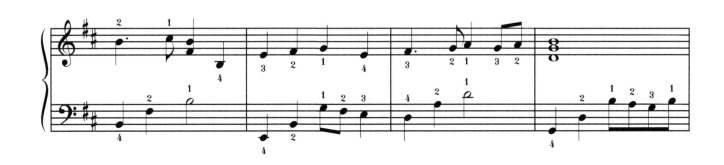

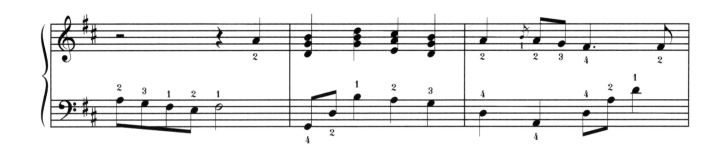

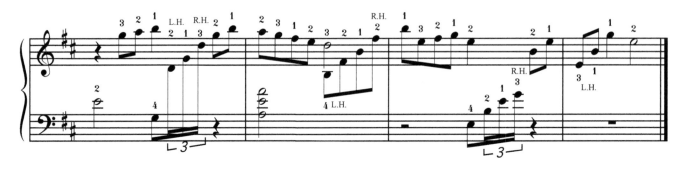

28

A Jig

Arr: Deborah Friou

R. Askue
16th c.

Quickly

29

Robin

Arr: Deborah Friou

Trad. English
16th c.

31

Lady Laiton's Almain

Arr: Deborah Friou

John Dowland
1563-1626

33

Bransle de la Torche

Harp Solo or Duet, First Part

Arr: Deborah Friou

Lever Harps: Set high C♯

Michael Praetorius
1612

34

Bransle de la Torche

Harp Duet: Second Part

Arr: Deborah Friou
Lever Harps: Set middle C♯

Michael Praetorius
1612

With Spirit

35

Bransle de Montirande

Harp Solo or Duet, First Part

Arr: Deborah Friou

Michael Praetorius
1612

Lever Harps: Set middle G♯ and middle and very low F♮

Moderately

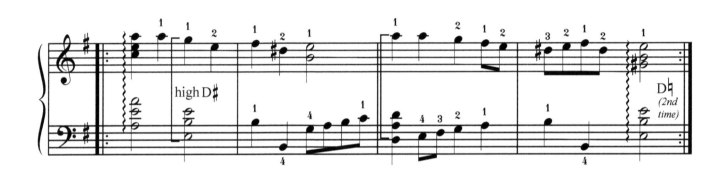

36

Bransle de Montirande

Harp Duet: Second Part

Arr: Deborah Friou

Michael Praetorius
1612

Moderately

Damp with flat palm

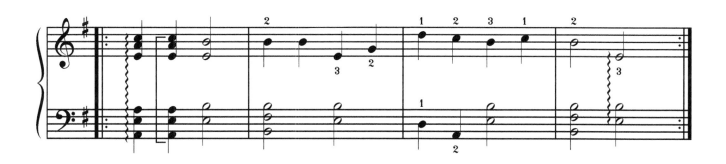

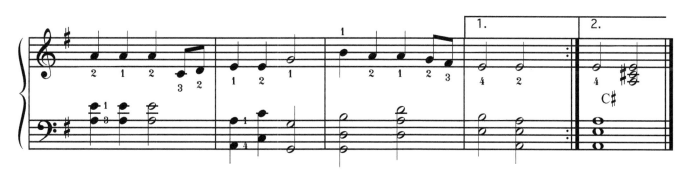

Courante CLXXXIII

Harp Solo or Duet, First Part

Arr: Deborah Friou

Michael Praetorius
1612

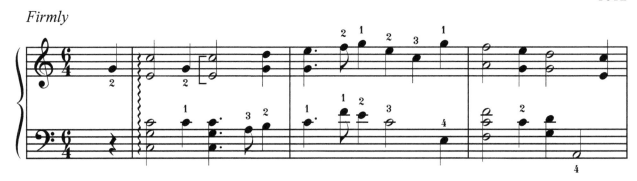

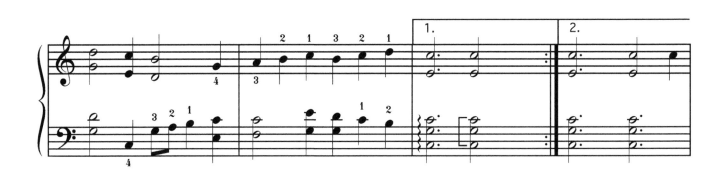

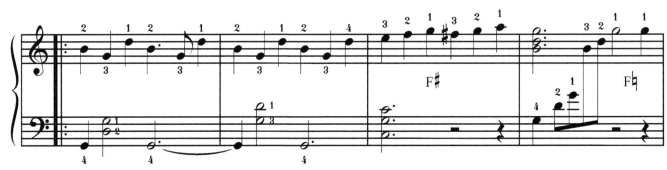

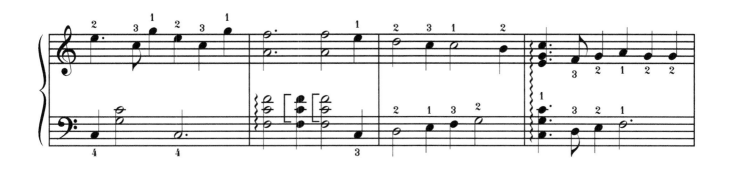

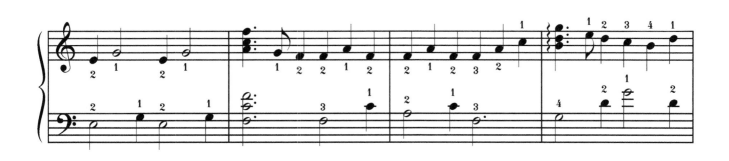

39

Courante CLXXXIII

Harp Duet: Second Part

Arr: Deborah Friou

Michael Praetorius
1612

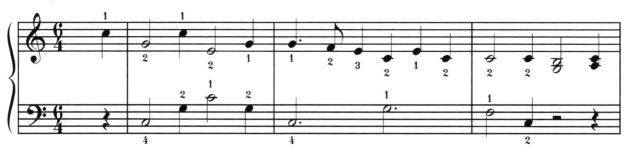

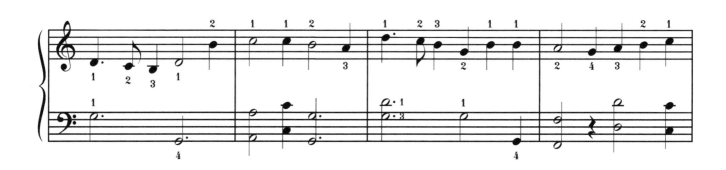

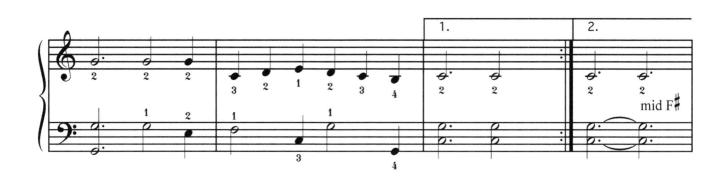

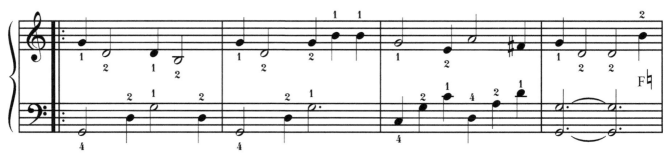

40

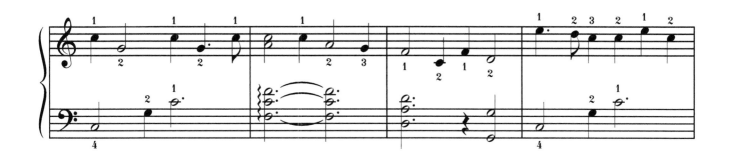

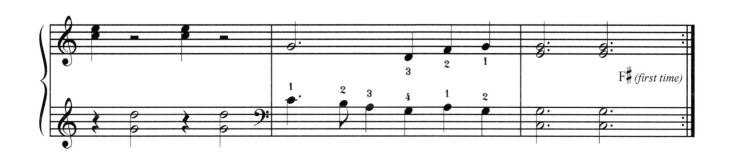

F♯ *(first time)*

La Rosette

Harp Solo or Duet, First Part

Arr: Deborah Friou

Michael Praetorius

1612

Lever Harps: Set middle G♯ and low F♮

With Spirit

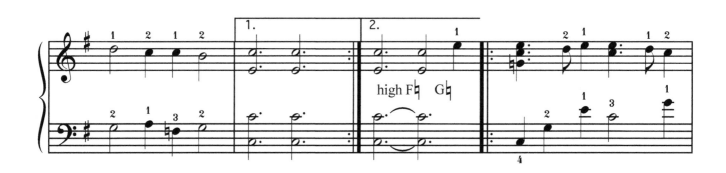

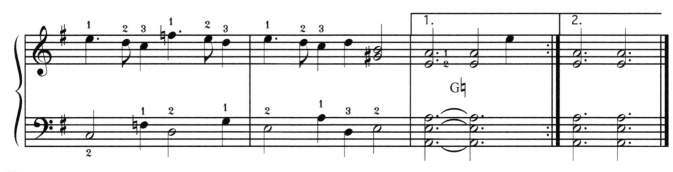

42

La Rosette

Harp Duet: Second Part

Arr: Deborah Friou

Michael Praetorius
1612

With Spirit

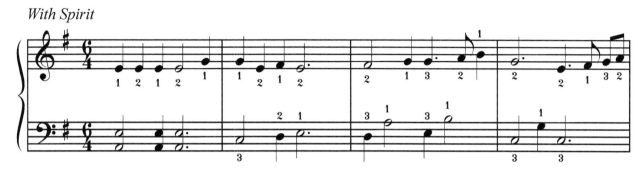

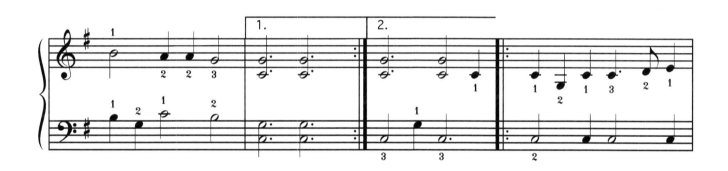

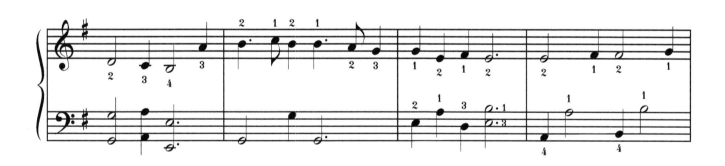

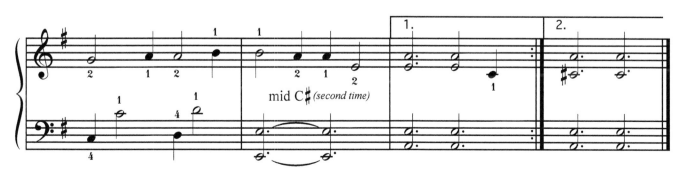

43

Courante XCVIII

Harp Solo or Duet, First Part

Arr: Deborah Friou

Michael Praetorius
1612

Flowing

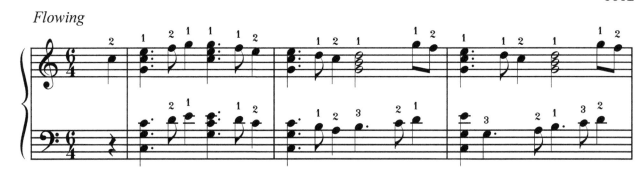

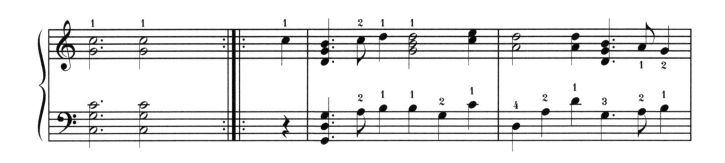

44

Courante XCVIII

Harp Duet: Second Part

Arr: Deborah Friou

Michael Praetorius
1612

Flowing

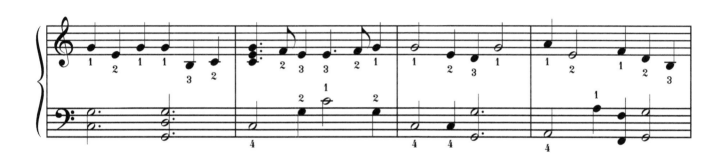

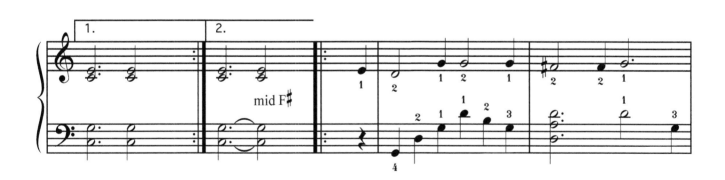

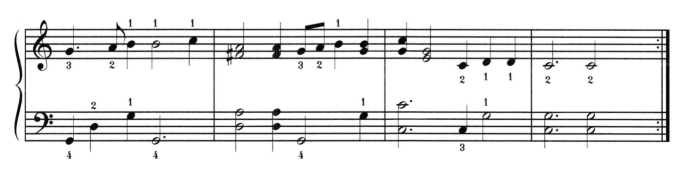

45

White Flowers

Arr: Deborah Friou

Anon. Italian
16th c.

left hand crosses over right

47

A harp recording that includes all of the music from this book is available on CD and as a download.

Please check online for:

Renaissance Muse
by
Deborah Friou

For information contact:

Friou Music
PO Box 157
Brunswick, ME 040111
USA